HERCULES

P9-AFL-892

WITHDRAWN

Sports Idols™

MARIA SHARAPOVA

Jason Glaser

WITHDRAWN

CONTRA COSTA COUNTY LIBRARY

PowerKiDS press.

3 1901 04370 4073

To my wife, Becky. Love-Love together forever.

Published in 2008 by The Rosen Publishing Group, Inc.
29 East 21st Street, New York, NY 10010

Copyright © 2008 by The Rosen Publishing Group, Inc.

All rights reserved. No part of this book may be reproduced in any form without permission in writing from the publisher, except by a reviewer.

First Edition

Editor: Amelie von Zumbusch
Book Design: Julio Gil
Photo Researcher: Nicole Pristash

Photo Credits: Cover, pp. 5, 7, 9, 11, 13, 15, 17, 19, 21 © Getty Images; cover (tennis ball) © Photodisc.

Library of Congress Cataloging-in-Publication Data

Glaser, Jason.
  Maria Sharapova / Jason Glaser. — 1st ed.
     p. cm. — (Sports idols)
  Includes index.
  ISBN 978-1-4042-4181-7 (library binding)
  1. Sharapova, Maria, 1987– —Juvenile literature. 2. Tennis players—Russia (Federation)—Biography—Juvenile literature. 3. Women tennis players—Russia (Federation)—Biography—Juvenile literature. I. Title.
  GV994.S47G53 2008
  796.342092—dc22
  [B]
                                                        2007025545

Manufactured in the United States of America

Contents

The Look of a Winner

Even without her tennis racket, Maria Sharapova would be hard to miss. For one thing, she stands 6 feet 2 inches (1.9 m) tall. Cameras snap pictures of her pretty face and bright smile.

Sharapova stands out even more on the tennis court. As she swings, she screams very loudly. The balls she hits fly as fast as 115 miles per hour (185 km/h). Her fans pack the stands when she plays. With each win, Sharapova gives them a lot to clap for. This young tennis star will keep winning for years to come.

Though Maria Sharapova generally holds her tennis racket in her right hand, she can also play very well left-handed.

Maria and the Tennis Stars

In 1986, Maria's parents lived in Gomel, in what is today Belarus. Then, an **accident** at a power plant in nearby Chernobyl spilled **radiation** over the land. Therefore, Maria's parents moved to Nyagan, in what is now Russia. Maria was born there on April 19, 1987. Soon after, Maria's family moved to Sochi, in present-day Russia. There, they became friends with a Russian tennis star who gave Maria her first racket.

Even as a child, Maria was good at tennis. Tennis star Martina Navratilova saw Maria play and suggested that she study tennis in America. When she was seven, Maria's father took her to America.

Maria's close friends and family, including her father, seen here, call her Masha. This is a Russian nickname for Maria.

Maria got a chance to show her skills to the Nick Bollettieri Tennis Academy, a tennis school in Bradenton, Florida. The teachers saw Maria's talent and gave her a scholarship. This means the academy gave Maria money so she could learn tennis and live at the school.

Other girls at the academy made fun of Maria because she could not speak English. Maria answered by trying to beat them at tennis. She began beating them in school **tournaments**. Maria won her first tournament in 2000. The next year, she won the Bollettieri Masters tournament. Winning this championship meant that Maria was the top student at the academy.

After winning the Bollettieri Masters tournament, Maria entered several tennis events. In March 2002, she took part in the junior girls singles event at the Nasdaq-100 Open.

Winning at Wimbledon

The rules of tennis keep young players from entering too many tournaments. Maria had to play hard to win her way into big events. The biggest tennis tournaments are the Australian Open, the French Open, the U.S. Open, and Wimbledon. By 2003, Maria had done well enough to play at each of them.

In 2004, Sharapova returned to Wimbledon and played great tennis. She won her way to the finals to face Serena Williams. Williams had won Wimbledon in 2002 and 2003. Sharapova beat Williams to become the second-youngest Wimbledon winner ever.

Sharapova won Wimbledon on July 3, 2004. As all Wimbledon winners do, she received a large, fancy plate as a trophy.

Number One at 18

In 2005, Sharapova turned 18 years old. She grew 2 inches (5 cm) that year and began having trouble playing. Her new size changed her swing. However, she was old enough to play in many more tournaments now. By playing more, Sharapova could get more points. The more points Sharapova had, the higher she moved in the **rankings**.

Sharapova scored points in big tournaments and won smaller tournaments. This way, she moved up fast in the rankings. On August 22, 2005, Sharapova became the number-one women's tennis player in the world. She was the first Russian-born woman to reach number one.

In August 2005, Sharapova held her first-place ranking for just a week. However, she was ranked first again in September and October of that year.

Some people thought Sharapova might let fame go to her head. She was working on lots of **commercials** and extra appearances. She fell out of her number-one ranking. Sharapova showed her doubters were wrong by winning four tournaments and beating strong players in big tournaments.

At the U.S. Open in 2006, Sharapova showed everyone how good she really was. She blasted her way to the final round. She faced Justine Henin, a player Sharapova had lost to many times. That day, she quickly beat Henin, and Sharapova won her second major, or important, tournament.

The U.S. Open takes place each year at the USTA Billie Jean King National Tennis Center in New York. Sharapova won the tournament there on September 9, 2006.

Million-Dollar Smile

Sharapova has to mix her tennis and her fame. The Bollettieri Academy is owned by a group of **agents**. In return for training there, Sharapova agreed to make deals with companies to show off their products, or goods. She even has her own brand of **perfume**! These deals make Sharapova the highest-paid female tennis player in the world.

However, Sharapova will not do that extra work around tournament time. She always makes time to practice. Sharapova reminded people that she is a skilled player who can play with the best by reaching the Australian Open finals in 2007.

One of the products Sharapova helps sell is a watch made by the company TAG Heuer. She showed off this watch at an event in New York City.

Off the Court

Sharapova says she thinks of herself as an ordinary girl. She loves to shop and eat sweet treats. She likes movies, music, and reading books. Sharapova also likes going to **spas** and dreaming up her own tennis clothes. Between practices, she likes doing **yoga**.

Some of Sharapova's friends call her a geek. She likes taking classes on the Internet. She thinks getting postage stamps is fun. Sharapova often giggles and hops around. When she won the U.S. Open, Sharapova danced wildly while holding the **trophy**. She was so wild the trophy top came off and fell to the ground!

Sharapova laughed when her wild dancing and jumping made the top of her U.S. Open trophy fall off in 2006.

Helping Others

In August 2006, Sharapova started the Maria Sharapova Foundation. This group gives money to help poor children follow their dreams. She has also helped raise money for people in Florida who have been hurt by bad storms called hurricanes.

Sharapova has not forgotten where she and her family came from. Many people who could not get away from Chernobyl became sick after the accident. People are still sick in that part of the world. In 2007, Sharapova gave $100,000 to help the people near Chernobyl. She also became a **goodwill ambassador** for the United Nations.

At the United Nations building in New York City, Sharapova presented her check to the United Nations Development Programme to help people near Chernobyl.

Sharapova has already won Wimbledon and the U.S. Open. Her dream is to win all the grand slam tournaments. To do this, she would also need to win the French Open and Australian Open. If she should win first place in the **Olympic Games**, she would have a "golden grand slam."

There will also be life after tennis. Sharapova does not want to play tennis much after turning 30. She has thoughts of building a business, working in **fashion**, writing books, or even acting. However, 30 is still a long way off for Sharapova. She has much tennis left to play!

Glossary

accident (AK-seh-dent) An unexpected thing that happens.

agents (AY-jents) People who help writers, actors, or players with their jobs.

commercials (kuh-MER-shulz) TV or radio messages trying to sell something.

fashion (FA-shun) The latest clothes.

goodwill ambassador (gud-WIL am-BA-suh-der) A person who helps a group called the United Nations care for the world's needy people.

Olympic Games (uh-LIM-pik GAYMZ) When the best sports players in the world meet every four years to play against each other.

perfume (per-FYOOM) Something used to make people smell good.

radiation (ray-dee-AY-shun) Rays of heat and light that are given off and can hurt people.

rankings (RAN-kingz) Measures of how well a player is doing in a sport.

spas (SPOZ) Places people go to for health and quiet.

tournaments (TOR-nuh-ments) Groups of games to decide the best player.

trophy (TROH-fee) A prize that is often shaped like a cup.

yoga (YOH-guh) A method of exercising and thinking deeply.

Index

A

accident, 6, 20

C

Chernobyl, 6, 20
court, 4

F

family, 6, 20
fans, 4
fashion, 22

G

Gomel, Belarus, 6

goodwill ambassador,
  20

N

Nyagan, Russia, 6

O

Olympic Games, 22

P

parents, 6
perfume, 16
power plant, 6

R

racket, 4, 6
radiation, 6
ranking(s), 12, 14

S

Sochi, Russia, 6
spas, 18

T

tournament(s), 8, 10,
  12, 14, 22
trophy, 18

Web Sites

Due to the changing nature of Internet links, PowerKids Press has developed an online list of Web sites related to the subject of this book. This site is updated regularly. Please use this link to access the list:
www.powerkidslinks.com/sidol/maria/

WITHDRAWN